THE
NICE PEOPLE

Henry Cuyler Bunner

[ZHINGOORA BOOKS]

This digital edition is published by Zhingoora Books.

The Cover is Designed by Pallav Sethiya.

THE NICE PEOPLE

"They certainly are nice people," I assented to my wife's observation, using the colloquial phrase with a consciousness that it was anything but "nice" English, "and I'll bet that their three children are better brought up than most of——"

" *Two* children," corrected my wife.

"Three, he told me."

"My dear, she said there were *two*."

"He said three."

"You've simply forgotten. I'm *sure* she told me they had only two—a boy and a girl."

"Well, I didn't enter into particulars."

"No, dear, and you couldn't have understood him. Two children."

"All right," I said; but I did not think it was all right. As a near-sighted man learns by enforced observation to recognize persons at a distance when the face is not visible to the normal eye, so the man with a bad memory learns, almost unconsciously, to listen carefully and report accurately. My memory is bad; but I had not had time to forget that Mr. Brewster Brede had told me that afternoon that he had three children, at present left in the care of his mother-in-law, while he and Mrs. Brede took their summer vacation.

"Two children," repeated my wife; "and they are staying with his aunt Jenny."

"He told me with his mother-in-law," I put in. My wife looked at me with a serious expression. Men may not remember much of what they are told about children; but any man knows the difference between an aunt and a mother-in-law.

"But don't you think they're nice people?" asked my wife.

"Oh, certainly," I replied. "Only they seem to be a little mixed up about their children."

"That isn't a nice thing to say," returned my wife. I could not deny it.

* * * * *

And yet, the next morning, when the Bredes came down and seated themselves opposite us at table, beaming and smiling in their natural, pleasant, well-bred fashion, I knew, to a social certainty, that they were "nice" people. He was a fine-looking fellow in his neat tennis-flannels, slim, graceful, twenty-eight or thirty years old, with a Frenchy pointed beard. She was "nice" in all her pretty clothes, and she herself was pretty with that type of prettiness which outwears most other types—the prettiness that lies in a rounded figure, a dusky skin, plump, rosy cheeks, white teeth and black eyes. She might have been twenty-five; you guessed that she was prettier than she was at twenty, and that she would be prettier still at forty.

And nice people were all we wanted to make us happy in Mr. Jacobus's summer boarding-house on top of Orange Mountain. For a week we had come down to breakfast each morning, wondering why we wasted the precious days of idleness with the company gathered around the Jacobus board. What joy of human companionship was to be had out of Mrs. Tabb and Miss Hoogencamp, the two middle-aged gossips from Scranton, Pa.—out of Mr. and Mrs. Biggle, an indurated head-bookkeeper and his prim and censorious wife—out of old Major Halkit, a retired business man, who, having once sold a few shares on commission, wrote for circulars of every stock company that was started, and tried to induce every one to invest who would listen to him? We looked around at those dull faces, the truthful indices of mean and barren minds, and decided that we would leave that morning. Then we ate Mrs. Jacobus's biscuit, light as Aurora's cloudlets, drank her honest coffee, inhaled the perfume of the late azaleas with which she decked her table, and decided to postpone our departure one more day. And then we wandered out to take our morning glance at what we called "our view"; and it seemed to us as if Tabb and Hoogencamp and Halkit and the Biggleses could not drive us away in a year.

I was not surprised when, after breakfast, my wife invited the Bredes to walk with us to "our view." The Hoogencamp-Biggle-Tabb-Halkit contingent never stirred off Jacobus's veranda; but we both felt that the Bredes would not profane that sacred scene. We strolled slowly across the fields, passed through the little belt of woods and, as I heard Mrs. Brede's little cry of startled rapture, I motioned to Brede to look up.

"By Jove!" he cried, "heavenly!"

We looked off from the brow of the mountain over fifteen miles of billowing green, to where, far across a far stretch of pale blue lay a dim purple line that we knew was Staten Island. Towns and villages lay before us and under us; there were ridges and hills, uplands and lowlands, woods and plains, all massed and mingled in that great silent sea of sunlit green. For silent it was to us, standing in the silence of a high place— silent with a Sunday stillness that made us listen, without taking thought, for the sound of bells coming up from the spires that rose above the tree-tops—the tree-tops that lay as far beneath us as the light clouds were above us that dropped great shadows upon our heads and faint specks of shade upon the broad sweep of land at the mountain's foot.

"And so that is *your* view?" asked Mrs. Brede, after a moment; "you are very generous to make it ours, too."

Then we lay down on the grass, and Brede began to talk, in a gentle voice, as if he felt the influence of the place. He had paddled a canoe, in his earlier days, he said, and he knew every river and creek in that vast stretch of landscape. He found his landmarks, and pointed out to us where the Passaic and the Hackensack flowed, invisible to us, hidden behind great ridges that in our sight were but combings of the green waves upon which we looked down. And yet, on the further side of those broad ridges and rises were scores of villages—a little world of country life, lying unseen under our eyes.

"A good deal like looking at humanity," he said; "there is such a thing as getting so far above our fellow men that we see only one side of them."

Ah, how much better was this sort of talk than the chatter and gossip of the Tabb and the Hoogencamp—than the Major's dissertations upon his everlasting circulars! My wife and I exchanged glances.

"Now, when I went up the Matterhorn" Mr. Brede began.

"Why, dear," interrupted his wife, "I didn't know you ever went up the Matterhorn."

"It—it was five years ago," said Mr. Brede, hurriedly. "I—I didn't tell you—when I was on the other side, you know—it was rather dangerous—well, as I was saying—it looked— oh, it didn't look at all like this."

A cloud floated overhead, throwing its great shadow over the field where we lay. The shadow passed over the mountain's brow and reappeared far below, a rapidly decreasing blot, flying eastward over the golden green. My wife and I exchanged glances once more.

Somehow, the shadow lingered over us all. As we went home, the Bredes went side by side along the narrow path, and my wife and I walked together.

"*Should you think*," she asked me, "that a man would climb the Matterhorn the very first year he was married?"

10

"I don't know, my dear," I answered, evasively; "this isn't the first year I have been married, not by a good many, and I wouldn't climb it—for a farm."

"You know what I mean," she said.

I did.

* * * * *

When we reached the boarding-house, Mr. Jacobus took me aside.

"You know," he began his discourse, "my wife she uset to live in N'
York!"

I didn't know, but I said "Yes."

"She says the numbers on the streets runs criss-cross-like.
Thirty-four's on one side o' the street an' thirty-five on t'other.
How's that?"

"That is the invariable rule, I believe."

"Then—I say—these here new folk that you 'n' your wife seem so mighty taken up with—d'ye know anything about 'em?"

"I know nothing about the character of your boarders, Mr. Jacobus," I replied, conscious of some irritability. "If I choose to associate with any of them——"

"Jess so—jess so!" broke in Jacobus. "I hain't nothin' to say ag'inst yer sosherbil'ty. But do ye *know* them?"

"Why, certainly not," I replied.

"Well—that was all I wuz askin' ye. Ye see, when *he* come here to take the rooms—you wasn't here then—he told my wife that he lived at number thirty-four in his street. An' yistiddy *she* told her that they lived at number thirty-five. He said he lived in an apartment-house. Now there can't be no apartment-house on two sides of the same street, kin they?"

"What street was it?" I inquired, wearily.

"Hundred 'n' twenty-first street."

"May be," I replied, still more wearily. "That's Harlem. Nobody knows what people will do in Harlem."

I went up to my wife's room.

"Don't you think it's queer?" she asked me.

"I think I'll have a talk with that young man to-night," I said, "and see if he can give some account of himself."

"But, my dear," my wife said, gravely, "*she* doesn't know whether they've had the measles or not."

"Why, Great Scott!" I exclaimed, "they must have had them when they were children."

"Please don't be stupid," said my wife. "I meant *their* children."

After dinner that night—or rather, after supper, for we had dinner in the middle of the day at Jacobus's—I walked down the long verandah to ask Brede, who was placidly smoking at the other end, to accompany me on a twilight stroll. Half way down I met Major Halkit.

"That friend of yours," he said, indicating the unconscious figure at the further end of the house, "seems to be a queer sort of a Dick. He told me that he was out of business, and just looking round for a chance to invest his capital. And I've been telling him what an everlasting big show he had to take stock in the Capitoline Trust Company—starts next month—four million capital—I told you all about it. 'Oh, well,' he says, 'let's wait and think about it.' 'Wait!' says I, 'the Capitoline Trust Company won't wait for *you*, my boy. This is letting you in on the ground floor,' says I, 'and it's now or never.' 'Oh, let it wait,' says he. I don't know what's in-*to* the man."

"I don't know how well he knows his own business, Major," I said as I started again for Brede's end of the veranda. But I was troubled none the less. The Major could not have influenced the sale of one share of stock in the Capitoline Company. But that stock was a great investment; a rare chance for a purchaser with a few thousand dollars. Perhaps it was no more remarkable that Brede should not invest than that I should not—and yet, it seemed to add one circumstance more to the other suspicious circumstances.

* * * * *

When I went upstairs that evening, I found my wife putting her hair to bed—I don't know how I can better describe an operation familiar to every married man. I waited until the last tress was coiled up, and then I spoke:

"I've talked with Brede," I said, "and I didn't have to catechize him. He seemed to feel that some sort of explanation was looked for, and he was very outspoken. You were right about the children—that is, I must have misunderstood him. There are only two. But the Matterhorn episode was simple enough. He didn't realize how dangerous it was until he had got so far into it that he couldn't back out; and he didn't tell her, because he'd left her here, you see, and under the circumstances——"

"Left her here!" cried my wife. "I've been sitting with her the whole afternoon, sewing, and she told me that he left her at Geneva, and came back and took her to Basle, and the baby was born there—now I'm sure, dear, because I asked her."

"Perhaps I was mistaken when I thought he said she was on this side of the water," I suggested, with bitter, biting irony.

"You poor dear, did I abuse you?" said my wife. "But, do you know, Mrs. Tabb said that *she* didn't know how many lumps of sugar he took in his coffee. Now that seems queer, doesn't it?"

It did. It was a small thing. But it looked queer, Very queer.

* * * * *

The next morning, it was clear that war was declared against the Bredes. They came down to breakfast somewhat late, and, as soon as they arrived, the Biggleses swooped up the last fragments that remained on their plates, and made a stately march out of the dining-room, Then Miss Hoogencamp arose and departed, leaving a whole fish-ball on her plate. Even as Atalanta might have dropped an apple behind her to tempt her pursuer to check his speed, so Miss Hoogencamp left that fish-ball behind her, and between her maiden self and contamination.

We had finished our breakfast, my wife and I, before the Bredes appeared. We talked it over, and agreed that we were glad that we had not been obliged to take sides upon such insufficient testimony.

After breakfast, it was the custom of the male half of the Jacobus household to go around the corner of the building and smoke their pipes and cigars where they would not annoy the ladies. We sat under a trellis covered with a grapevine that had borne no grapes in the memory of man. This vine, however, bore leaves, and these, on that pleasant summer morning, shielded from us two persons who were in earnest conversation in the straggling, half-dead flower-garden at the side of the house.

"I don't want," we heard Mr. Jacobus say, "to enter in no man's *pry*-vacy; but I do want to know who it may be, like, that I hev in my house. Now what I ask of *you*, and I don't want you to take it as in no ways *personal*, is—hev you your merridge-license with you?"

"No," we heard the voice of Mr. Brede reply. "Have you yours?"

I think it was a chance shot; but it told all the same. The Major (he was a widower) and

Mr. Biggle and I looked at each other; and Mr. Jacobus, on the other side of the grape-trellis, looked at—I don't know what—and was as silent as we were.

Where is *your* marriage-license, married reader? Do you know? Four men, not including Mr. Brede, stood or sat on one side or the other of that grape-trellis, and not one of them knew where his marriage-license was. Each of us had had one—the Major had had three. But where were they? Where is *yours?* Tucked in your best-man's pocket; deposited in his desk—or washed to a pulp in his white waistcoat (if white waistcoats be the fashion of the hour), washed out of existence—can you tell where it is? Can you— unless you are one of those people who frame that interesting document and hang it upon their drawing-room walls?

Mr. Brede's voice arose, after an awful stillness of what seemed like five minutes, and was, probably, thirty seconds:

"Mr. Jacobus, will you make out your bill at once, and let me pay it? I shall leave by the six o'clock train. And will you also send the wagon for my trunks?"

"I hain't said I wanted to hev ye leave——" began Mr. Jacobus; but Brede cut him short.

"Bring me your bill."

"But," remonstrated Jacobus, "ef ye ain't——"

"Bring me your bill!" said Mr. Brede.

* * * * *

My wife and I went out for our morning's walk. But it seemed to us, when we looked at "our view," as if we could only see those invisible villages of which Brede had told us— that other side of the ridges and rises of which we catch no glimpse from lofty hills or from the heights of human self-esteem. We meant to stay out until the Bredes had taken their departure; but we returned just in time to see Pete, the Jacobus darkey, the blacker of boots, the brasher of coats, the general handy-man of the house, loading the Brede trunks on the Jacobus wagon.

And, as we stepped upon the verandah, down came Mrs. Brede, leaning on Mr. Brede's arm, as though she were ill; and it was clear that she had been crying. There were heavy rings about her pretty black eyes.

My wife took a step toward her.

"Look at that dress, dear," she whispered; "she never thought anything like this was going to happen when she put *that* on."

It was a pretty, delicate, dainty dress, a graceful, narrow-striped affair. Her hat was trimmed with a narrow-striped silk of the same colors—maroon and white—and in her hand she held a parasol that matched her dress.

"She's had a new dress on twice a day," said my wife, "but that's the prettiest yet. Oh, somehow—I'm *awfully* sorry they're going!"

But going they were. They moved toward the steps. Mrs. Brede looked toward my wife, and my wife moved toward Mrs. Brede. But the ostracized woman, as though she felt the deep humiliation of her position, turned sharply away, and opened her parasol to shield her eyes from the sun. A shower of rice—a half-pound shower of rice—fell down over her pretty hat and her pretty dress, and fell in a spattering circle on the floor, outlining her skirts—and there it lay in a broad, uneven band, bright in the morning sun.

Mrs. Brede was in my wife's arms, sobbing as if her young heart would break.

"Oh, you poor, dear, silly children!" my wife cried, as Mrs. Brede sobbed on her shoulder, "why *didn't* you tell us?"

"W-W-W-We didn't want to be t-t-taken for a b-b-b-b-bridal couple," sobbed Mrs. Brede; "and we d-d-didn't *dream* what awful lies we'd have to tell, and all the aw-awful mixed-up-ness of it. Oh, dear, dear, dear!"

* * * * *

"Pete!" commanded Mr. Jacobus, "put back them trunks. These folks stays here's long's they wants ter. Mr. Brede"—he held out a large, hard hand—"I'd orter've known better," he said. And my last doubt of Mr. Brede vanished as he shook that grimy hand in manly fashion.

The two women were walking off toward "our view," each with an arm about the other's waist—touched by a sudden sisterhood of sympathy.

"Gentlemen," said Mr. Brede, addressing Jacobus, Biggle, the Major and me, "there is a hostelry down the street where they sell honest New Jersey beer. I recognize the obligations of the situation."

23

We five men filed down the street. The two women went toward the pleasant slope where the sunlight gilded the forehead of the great hill. On Mr. Jacobus's veranda lay a spattered circle of shining grains of rice. Two of Mr. Jacobus's pigeons flew down and picked up the shining grains, making grateful noises far down in their throats.

End of the book.